MARINE MAMMAL
PRESERVATION

PEGGY THOMAS

MARINE MAMMAL PRESERVATION

The Science of Saving Animals

TWENTY-FIRST CENTURY BOOKS
BROOKFIELD, CONNECTICUT

FOR MY KATE AND ALL THE
WHALE WATCHERS
FROM MIDDLEPORT ELEMENTARY

Acknowledgments
I'd like to thank everyone who helped in the research of this book, especially John Dayton, Greg Early, and Sonia Mumford at the New England Aquarium; Tom Pitchford at the Marine Mammal Pathology Lab in Florida; and Andrew Johnson, director of the Sea Otter Research and Conservation Program at the Monterey Bay Aquarium.

Cover photograph courtesy of © Gerry Ellis/ENP Images

Photographs courtesy of Minden Pictures: pp. 6 (© Gerry Ellis), 14 (© Flip Nicklin), 16 (Michio Hoshino), 23 (© Flip Nicklin), 29 (© Flip Nicklin), 34 (© Frans Lanting), 38 (© Tim Fitzharris), 43 (© Fred Bavendam), 48 (© Flip Nicklin), 52 (bottom © Flip Nicklin), 54 (© Flip Nicklin); © 2000 www.norbertwu.com: pp. 10 (Norbert Wu), 15 (Bob Cranston), 46 (Norbert Wu), 57 (Peter Howorth); © New England Aquarium: pp. 19 (Paul Erickson), 31, 33 (Eric Rowe), 55 (Chris Slay); Laura Gerstein: p. 25; © Carol "Krill" Carson: p. 27; © Monterey Bay Aquarium/Randy Wilder: p. 36; Florida Marine Research Institute: pp. 40, 44; Peter Arnold, Inc.: pp. 49 (© Gunter Ziesler), 52 (top © Still Pictures)

The Library of Congress Control Number: 00-030223
0-7613-1458-X (lib. bdg.)

Published by Twenty-First Century Books
A Division of The Millbrook Press, Inc.
2 Old New Milford Road
Brookfield, Connecticut 06804
www.millbrookpress.com

CONTENTS

A sea otter floating in a kelp bed inspects its foot.

1 MAN AND MARINE MAMMALS

A female manatee poked her nose out of the water for a breath of air, her nostrils looking like two of the holes in a bowling ball. She was huge, yet hidden in the murky water. Her calf nuzzled against her side as she fed on the lush sea grass growing along the edge of the canal.

They seemed so peaceful, unaware of the dangerous world they lived in. Just a few yards away, a family fished from the canal wall with baited hooks, litter blew in the wind, and boats cruised noisily out to open water. This was the home of one of the most endangered marine mammals in the United States.

FUR, FLIPPERS, FINS

There are more than 100 different types of marine mammals living in the seas. They range in size from a sea otter the size of a bassett hound to the largest living creature on Earth, the blue whale. Some are placid like the manatee, and some are predatory like the killer whale.

The words "marine mammal" take in a wide array of animals, including cetaceans (whales, dolphins, and porpoises); pinnipeds (seals, sea lions, and walruses); sirenia (manatees and dugongs); and sea otters. Like their landlubber cousins, marine mammals are warm-blooded, breathe through lungs, give birth to live young, and feed their infants milk. Their skeletons reveal their evolution from land animals to sea creatures millions of years ago. Sea otters retained a tail, four limbs, and grasping front paws, and seals still have fingernails. Even whales have "finger" bones in their fins.

Marine mammals share with us a distant terrestrial past, and we have been connected ever since. As hunter and hunted, we are linked in a common food chain, and our paths cross frequently in ocean ecosystems.

TROUBLE AT SEA

Long before plastics, lightbulbs, and other modern inventions, people relied on marine mammals for food, tools, and clothing. Their meat was good to eat, and almost every part of the body could be utilized. Seal and sea lion skin was strong, waterproof material for housing and clothing; sea otter furs, the densest in the world, were made into lovely coats.

A wealth of products could be made from a whale. Its oil, boiled down from blubber, could light lamps, lubricate machinery, make candles, soap, and crayons. A waxy substance called spermaceti was used in cosmetics and skin cleansers. Teeth and bones were made into jewelry and buttons. Baleen made corset stays and buggy whips. Tendons were turned into tennis racket strings and surgical thread, and whale skin became shoelaces and saddles.

Over time, the greed for whale parts grew. Hunting techniques and equipment became more efficient and sophisticated. Many whale species hovered on the brink of extinction. Between 1785 and 1939, some 40,000 southern right whales were killed. Today, there are about 3,000 left. Sea otters once thrived along the Pacific Coast from Baja California north to Alaska, across the Aleutian Islands to northern Japan. Over a 140-year period, they were hunted to near extinction; only small isolated groups survived. The population along the California coast fell from 20,000 to less than 50. Today, the population hovers around 2,000. Although hunting still occurs, marine mammals face more pressing threats from pollution, entanglement in fishing equipment, habitat degradation, and collisions with ships.

Since the first marine mammals slipped into the sea, they have followed the ocean currents teeming with life. Men in ships follow and fish in these same paths, putting themselves on an inevitable collision course with whales. Garbage bags, plastic bottles, and other debris, as well as chemical pollutants, are spread across the globe by the same ocean currents. Researchers have reported seeing floating children's balloons more than 200 miles (322 kilometers) from land. Marine mammals frequently mistake these bits of plastic and rubber for jellyfish and eat them.

Agricultural runoff, toxic chemicals, industrial waste, and untreated sewage also pour into the water supply. If these chemicals aren't good for us to drink, bathe in, and swim in, imagine what it would be like to live in that water your whole life. Although many of the chemicals such as DDT have been banned in North America, they still move throughout ecosystems and the food chain. Sitting at the top of the food chain, marine mammals act as important environmental indicators, a measurement of the health of the oceans. If marine mammals are in trouble, so is the rest of the ecosystem.

Most people don't think that beach development could affect marine mammals, but it does. Seals, sea lions, and walruses need land to survive, and with the growing human population clamoring for shoreline, there are fewer and fewer beaches for pupping, nursing, and molting. On the rare occasions that a seal hauls out onto a tourist beach, it might be shooed away, or worse, harassed. Educating the public to the normal behavior of seals is necessary for these species' survival.

Just off shore, miles and miles of hooked fishing lines and nets crisscross the oceans. The U.S. Marine Mammal Commission estimates that there are more than 25,000 miles (40,250 kilometers) of

An otter eats the soft center of a sea urchin. Otters play a valu-able role in protecting the kelp beds by eating urchins and other animals that eat the kelp roots, called holdfasts.

Food-Chain Reaction

Overfishing can set off a food-chain reaction. A study in the Bering Sea showed that the decline in the fish population meant fewer fish for seals and sea lions to feed on, so their population fell. Killer whales, whose favorite food was the seal, were forced to find another food source, and switched to eating sea otters. As a result, the troubled sea otter population in the Aleutian Islands declined by 90 percent in less than ten years.

A decline in sea otters caused a population boom for the sea otter's favorite food, the sea urchin. These spiny invertebrates feed on seaweed called kelp. They ate significant portions of the kelp beds, destroying many other animals' habitat and food source. Even you eat kelp. It's harvested and turned into a powder called alginate, which is used as a thickener in ice cream, toothpaste, and other products.

net used in the sea—enough to encircle the entire planet. Hundreds of thousands of cetaceans, pinnipeds, sea otters, and birds are caught and snagged in nets and drown each year. They are called bycatch because they are caught unintentionally. But the number of accidental deaths is devastating to the populations.

PROTECTIVE POLICIES

By the early 1900s, a few international policies were created to protect marine species. The International Fur Seal Treaty of 1911 stopped widespread slaughter of both seals and the California sea otter. But policies and laws were made because governments were concerned that the decreasing animal populations were affecting the economy, not because they jeopardized a species' survival.

In 1946, 14 countries formed the International Whaling Commission to manage whale populations as an economic resource. Forty years later, they declared a moratorium, or a ban, on commercial whaling. However, commission membership is voluntary, and nations routinely apply for special permission to take whales for scientific research and native subsistence. Unfortunately, Japan, Norway, and Iceland continue to argue and defy the ban. Unlike most land animals, marine mammals live in international waters, moving in and out of nations' borders. Laws designed to protect them are extremely difficult to enforce.

The United States government adopted the Marine Mammal Protection Act in 1972, declaring that it is illegal to hunt or harass any marine mammal in U.S. waters. Here again are exceptions for native subsistence hunting, research, education, display, and accidental bycatch of the fishing industry.

Laws by themselves are not effective deterrents. The habitats of marine mammals need to be preserved. But for many animals, not enough information is known about their lives, habitat usage, and threats to their survival to create adequate conservation plans. The beluga whale, for example, is listed in the International Union for the Conservation of Nature and Natural Resources

(IUCN)/World Conservation Union's "insufficiently known" category, which means more information is needed before politics can offer protection.

Who provides the necessary data to create conservation laws? Marine biologists, researchers in pathology and ecology, as well as scientists who work with sound and satellites, all do. Not just one field of study can offer solutions to problems that have taken centuries to create. Some scientists perch over the bow of a ship poised with a specially rigged crossbow, while others are poised over the eyepiece of a microscope. Some researchers work one animal at a time, and others deal with an entire species. But they all have one goal in mind—to keep marine mammals swimming free.

2 GOING ON A WHALE WATCH

Imagine looking out over the railing of a research ship and all you can see are miles and miles of water on all sides. The animals you have come out to study live beneath it, but they only come to the surface occasionally to breathe. How could you possibly find one whale, seal, or sea lion?

The marine mammals' watery habitat makes them extremely difficult to study. Biologists can't follow the animal's every move without scuba gear or deep diving equipment. It's an exhausting game of hide-and-seek, where you rarely see the other team.

We can only imagine what it feels like to dive half a mile below the surface like an elephant seal, or to migrate from the Northern Hemisphere to the Southern Hemisphere like the gray whale. But innovative technologies, such as satellite telemetry or tracking, allow scientists to learn more about marine mammals than ever before.

Each time a humpback dives deep into the ocean, it lifts its tail high out of the water. That's when the photographer snaps its mug shot. Researchers also record the whale's location and behavior and enter each sighting in an extensive catalog, like the North Atlantic Humpback Whale Catalog kept by Allied Whale at the College of the Atlantic in Bar Harbor, Maine. Some whales have a more extensive file than others. One female, named Salt, has been observed for more than 15 years.

Dozens of research institutions collect photographs and behavioral data for the catalog, which so far contains more than 5,200 individual humpback whales and fills more than 15 three-ring binders. Knowing the size of a population tells scientists whether

The distinctive markings on whales' tails let researchers keep track of individual whales.

they are dealing with an endangered species or one that is on the road to recovery. Fortunately, the humpback population of the North Atlantic is thriving, but the endangered northern right whale population is barely holding its own.

Before the 1980s, no one knew where the small group of right whales went after they left their summer feeding grounds in the Bay of Fundy off Newfoundland. By using photo ID, researchers proved that those same whales spent the winter off the coast of Georgia and Florida in an area riddled with shipping traffic. This type of information led to the development of conservation plans in both areas of their critical habitats.

The right whale project welcomes all the help it can get and gladly accepts good quality and well-documented whale photographs from boaters and fishermen. Each photo goes through a thorough examination before being included. Three researchers at the New England Aquarium, where the Northern Right Whale Catalog is kept, independently compare the amateur photographs to the ones in the catalog. If all three researchers match a photograph with the same whale, then the photo and the sighting information becomes part of the official record. Today, there are more than 350 northern right whales represented in the files.

SEAL SURVEILLANCE

Where do these animals go when they dive below the surface? A camera can't help answer that kind of question, but a satellite can.

Satellites orbit the earth several times each day receiving and sending military, scientific, and communications signals. The satellites used by the National Oceanographic and Atmospheric Administration (NOAA) to follow weather patterns are also fitted with ARGOS instruments that can locate the source of data from a transmitter anywhere on the globe. The ARGOS system is used by researchers all over the world to track wild animals.

By attaching a transmitter, called a tag, to a marine mammal, researchers can plot on a map where the animal goes, record how deep it dives, and how long it stays on the surface. A transmitter is a mini radio about the size of a pocket pager, weighing between 5.25 and 10.5 ounces (150 to 300 grams). It sends a signal that is picked up by a satellite passing more than 621 miles (1,000 kilometers) overhead. The signal can't penetrate water, so the tag transmits each time the animal surfaces. The information is sent to the satellite by digital code, which is then beamed down to a processing station on the ground. The readout looks like a college level math exam, but each number means something. Greg Early, research scientist at the New England Aquarium, monitors the animals that the aquarium rehabilitates and releases. He can check up on each animal from his office. "Once a day I get an E-mail from the ground station that tells me if we got any readings or not."

THAT'S A LOVELY TRANSMITTER YOU'RE WEARING

Transmitters are basically the same inside and can be designed to collect date, time, longitude, latitude, dive depths, dive duration, and other data. But how the transmitter is attached is different for every animal.

A seal or sea lion has the tag glued to the fur on the back of its neck. When the seal molts, the tag falls off.

Manatees wear their tags dragging along like a bride's train. It is attached by a long tether with a loop around the animal's tail. The tether allows the transmitter to float at the surface, providing maximum transmission time.

Sea otters are so frisky that researchers have found it's best to implant their transmitters under the skin.

Whales don't sit still for glue and are too powerful to drag their tags, so they are attached by sticking a barb into the blubber layer just behind the blowhole. A marksman fires the barb into the skin with a compound crossbow. Because many whales lose their transmitters after only a few days, designers are constantly looking for new ways to make them work for longer periods of time and stay on better.

After its rehabilitation, this harbor seal is being released by New England Aquarium staff with a satellite tag attached behind its head. It will add to what researchers know about the habits of seals.

Once a transmitter is in place it would seem that all systems are go, but many things can go wrong—transmitters mysteriously fail, batteries die, glue or barbs come undone, or a satellite could get hit by a meteor. Even when the device is working well, there are no guarantees that there will be a lot of information transmitted. Tags only transmit when they are above water, and marine mammals spend most of their time below the surface. Couple that with the fact that the satellites only pick up the signal when they are overhead. The animal must be at the surface the same time the satellite passes for there to be a successful transmission. Early estimates,

"There are only about 20 to 30 chances to locate your animal a day."

A factor in the longevity of the transmitter is the size of the battery. The larger the animal, the larger the battery can be. Some tags can give daily messages for up to a year. Smaller ones last about 100 days. But that's enough time to know if a newly released animal has the ability to survive.

KEEPING IN TOUCH

"The basic question we're trying to answer is what happens to a rehabilitated animal after we let it go," said Early. "We can point the animal in the right direction, but they tend to go wherever they want to go."

The first time the aquarium used satellite technology to track a seal was on a nearly 600-pound (272-kilogram) hooded seal nicknamed Stephanie. In February 1996, Stephanie was stranded in Nahant, Massachusetts. After several months of veterinary care at the aquarium, Stephanie was released, and for the first time showed scientists and the world a rare glimpse into the mysterious life of a hooded seal. When Stephanie galumphed off the beach and into the water, her transmitter indicated that she headed north to the Arctic. The transmitter relayed messages for nine months, and told scientists that at one time she dove more than 3,000 feet (915 meters) deep, and rarely came out onto land or ice.

Most released animals are tracked for about 100 days. "Seals that don't seem to be able to survive have trouble in the first three weeks," Early said. "We hope they'll go back to being normal seals, able to forage and feed themselves." By looking at the dive behavior, how often and how deep they go, Early can infer that a seal is actively looking for food and finding it. But future technology may give scientists a more direct measure of the animal's feeding patterns.

Temperature sensors originally developed for use on astronauts may someday be used on seals. These sensors are small enough to fit into a pill that the animal swallows. Seals feed on cold fish, and by looking at the fluctuations of the seal's stomach temperature, scientists would know when a seal was feeding. But the technology has not yet caught up with a researcher's desire to answer certain questions. No one has designed a sensor to work off a satellite . . . yet.

North Atlantic Right Whale (*Eubalaena glacialis*)

This whale was called the right whale by whalers because it was the right whale to hunt. It swam slowly at the surface making it easy to kill, and the carcass floated conveniently at the surface instead of sinking to the bottom of the ocean like other whales. It was hunted to near extinction.

The right whale feeds on tiny creatures called copepods and krill, and scoops up giant mouthfuls of water and strains it out through long fringed plates called baleen. An adult whale eats between 2,000 and 5,000 pounds (908 and 2,270 kilograms) of food a day. It grows to be 45 to 55 feet (14 to 17 meters) long and weighs 70 tons (63.5 tonnes). Right whales have no dorsal fin and have two widely separated blowholes that make a V-shape spout. They are closely related to the South Atlantic right whale that lives in the Southern Hemisphere. There are an estimated 300 northern right whales left.

3 CLICK . . . CLACK . . . RUMBLE . . . PING!

"Low, almost imperceptible sounds that resonated through the ocean like a Gregorian chant . . . each call a long, low rumble that was so unfamiliar to my ears that at first I thought it was an electronic artifact or shipping noise." That's how Dr. Christopher Clark described the voice of the blue whale, the largest animal in the world, when he first heard it in 1993. "I froze because I realized that the whale whose voice was responsible for . . . the faint regular hum in my ears was about 500 miles away!"

Dr. Clark is the director of the Marine Mammal Research Program at Cornell Bioacoustics Research Lab where he studies animal sounds—how they are created, what they are used for, and what the sounds reveal about an animal's behavior.

It makes sense to use sound to study marine mammals because sound travels up to five times faster in water than in air. Marine mammals are built to use sound to communicate, navigate, and locate prey.

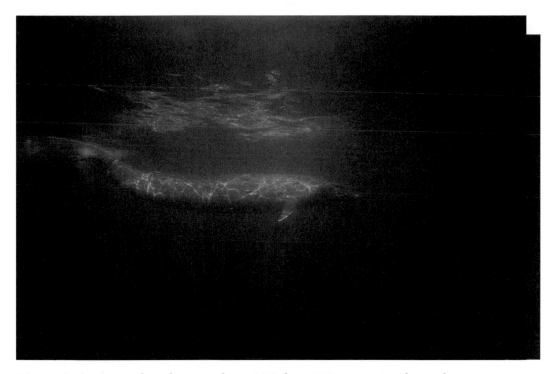

Blue whales are often longer than 100 feet (30 meters)—if you know someone 5 feet (152 centimeters) tall you would have to lie 20 of them in a row to reach that length.

Toothed whales such as dolphins and sperm whales emit a click every second or so to detect prey or obstacles. The sound is made by vibrating the air that is locked within the whale's nasal passages. The vibrations are then funneled out through the skull bone and the melon, the specialized sac in the forehead. The melon can be reshaped in order to direct the signal. The whales listen to the echoes of the clicks as the sound bounces off objects. This system of navigation is called echolocation. The military has studied marine mammal echolocation for decades and has even designed submarine sonar systems that mimic the whale's melon.

Each species of cetacean has its own vocabulary of squeaks, clicks, and groans that bioacoustics experts are learning to identify. The calls of belugas have been described as sounding like insect shrills, rain forest birdsong, a snake's rattle, and a cow passing wind. Sperm whales emit a click and clank like a jail cell door slamming shut, and the humpback's song groans and rumbles like distant thunder and squeals like a guinea pig being squeezed. No matter how strange the sounds may seem to amateurs, experts are able to detect patterns, decipher behaviors, and in the future identify individual whales as they vocalize.

Some of the loudest vocalizations come from the blue whale, which produces a sound measured at 190 decibels in water. Its extremely deep voice travels easily through the ocean's deep sound channels, allowing blue whales to communicate with each other over hundreds of thousands of square miles. Blue whales calling off the coast of Newfoundland, for example, can be heard as far south as the West Indies. Clark speculates that this long distance dialogue may not only help the whale communicate with other whales far away, but may also be used to map out its environment over hundreds of miles of underwater terrain.

HARD ON THE EARS?

Cetaceans not only make a vast array of sounds, they can hear frequencies that we cannot. Dolphins, for example, can hear frequencies of up to 150,000 hertz, while the typical person can only hear up to 20,000 hertz. But does the sensitive hearing of marine mammals make them more vulnerable to underwater noise pollution? That's what Clark was asked to study for the Acoustic Thermometry of Ocean Climate Project (ATOC).

ATOC planned to send sound waves through the Pacific Ocean to take the ocean's temperature in an experiment to study the ocean's heat content. Sound travels faster in warm water than in cold water, so by measuring the time it takes the sound to travel between two underwater points, scientists can figure out the average temperature along that path.

When ATOC announced their plan, conservationists quickly sounded their alarm and requested a study to see how marine mammals would be affected by such noise. But the seas are already

A manatee, which Ed Gerstein named Stormy, pushing the striped paddle. The manatees rest their head in the hoop at left to listen to different noises.

Hearing Tests for Manatees

Most people think that manatees are too slow to get out of a boat's way, but Ed Gerstein, director of marine mammal research at Florida Atlantic University, doesn't agree. He thinks that the manatee's hearing may be the problem. He devised an experiment where he trained captive manatees to respond to underwater recordings of a wide range of sounds.

The manatees were shown how to push a striped paddle if they heard a sound, and to push a solid-colored paddle if they didn't. They were rewarded with pellets of monkey chow. It turns out that the manatees could hear high-pitched sounds that were in the same range as their own chirping vocalizations. Boat engine noises are below or near the bottom of their hearing range, which means that a manatee would not normally hear a boat until it is about 50 feet (15 meters) away. Gerstein proposed that all boats be fitted with a device that broadcasts a high frequency to warn off manatees and prevent collisions, the number one cause of death among manatees.

filled with all sorts of sound, some natural, some man-made. The drone of ship engines, the blast of underwater drilling, and other clamor of military sonar and scientific experiments all add to the underwater din.

To measure the effect of the ATOC sound on marine mammals, a loudspeaker that emits a low-frequency sound was lowered 3,200 feet (976 meters) beneath the ocean. Sound was transmitted for 20 minutes every four hours. The marine mammals in the area were tracked before and after transmission to see how they were affected. One hypothesis stated that animals in distress would swim away from the speakers. Statistical results indicated that some whales do stay further away, but didn't abandon their habitat.

COUNTING WHALES

The developments in bioacoustics research and specially designed computer software have revolutionized marine mammal studies, offering new ways to answer questions that have nagged biologists for decades, like how do you accurately count whales?

The answer: with your ears, not just your eyes. That was the consensus after a 1995 study to compare two methods of counting whales from a moving ship. Traditionally, biologists stood on deck and counted each animal they saw at the surface. But one researcher likened this method to looking for birds in a dark forest with your ears plugged. Most of the time the study animal is hidden from view, and if you blink you could miss its brief appearance. But as bird watchers have learned, you can find more animals by listening.

Clark and his crew dropped a series, or an array, of underwater microphones called hydrophones, spaced about ten miles apart, into the water along the coast of California. Each hydrophone records the clicks and groans of a nearby whale at slightly different times. The sound is recorded first by the hydrophone nearest to the whale, and then a fraction of a second later by more distant hydrophones and on down the line. From the difference in arrival time between any two hydrophones, scientists can calculate a bearing line that points at the whale. By repeating this process for each pair of hydrophones, they get lines that intersect at the whale's location. Specially designed computer software measures the time delays and calculates the whale's position. This is called time-difference fixing.

Kurt Fristrup, at left, holds part of the magnetic release for a pop-up hydrophone. It's called that because, in addition to a radio-triggered release system, the hydrophone container also has a release that will fire on a predetermined day, and since they float, it will "pop up" to the surface.

The ship also towed a mile-long cable fixed with 16 hydrophones. Observers stood on deck recording all the whales they saw during daylight hours, while below deck the acoustic team manned multichannel tape recorders and computers listening to the vocalizations of marine mammals picked up by the towed hydrophones.

The result showed that blue whales were detected six times more often, and fin whales three times more often by sound than by sight. However, not all whales were heard either. Eight blue whales were seen from the ship but did not vocalize. Both sight and sound are necessary for a more accurate count.

SOUNDING THE ALARM

One more man-made sound in the sea is the periodic ping of acoustical alarms that warn porpoises and other marine mammals that fishing nets are near. Dr. Jon Lien of Newfoundland's Memorial University developed the acoustical alarm to keep humpback whales out of cod traps. After a year of experimenting with different devices and different sounds, he found one that humpbacks avoided.

The idea of an underwater alarm isn't new; NASA developed a similar device to be attached to payloads that landed in the sea. The pinger was able to withstand heavy hits and emitted a signal for hours on end. They are now rigged to the "black box" flight recorders of airplanes. But pingers for porpoises and other marine mammals was a novel, yet simple idea, one that significantly reduced bycatch and was easily adaptable to fishermen's nets.

An experiment conducted by Scott Kraus of the New England Aquarium revealed that nets with pingers caught 95 percent fewer porpoises. Over a span of two months only two porpoises were caught in 421 nets rigged with pingers, compared to 25 porpoises caught in 423 nets fixed with fake silent pingers.

Fishermen all over the world now use pingers on their nets. Some fishermen in California heard the good news and rigged their nets with a similar device they purchased at Radio Shack. The alarms beeped like a truck backing up, but they worked. Porpoises heard the alarm and avoided the nets. These sausage-shaped pingers are programmed to ping just loud enough to be heard from at least 328 feet (100 meters) away underwater, just enough time for a whale or dolphin to change course.

Today, all drift-net fishermen in California and Oregon, and fishermen who use sink nets in New England, are required to use them. So far, deaths of whales and dolphins have dropped by two thirds on the West Coast. Conservationists in New Zealand are hoping that pingers will be just as successful in keeping their most endangered dolphin, the Hector's dolphin, from becoming entangled in gill nets. There are only 4,000 to 5,000 of these small coastal cetaceans left, and they are very vulnerable to entanglements.

Scientists still are not sure why the pingers work so well, or if the success will continue. More studies will be needed to find out if there are any long-term effects. But so far, the pinger is a welcome sound in the sea.

A Hector's dolphin

Hector's Dolphin (*Cephalorhynchus hectori*)

These striking black, white, and gray dolphins are found only off the coast of New Zealand, and were named after New Zealand explorer and naturalist Sir James Hector. They are small, 5 to 6 feet (1.5 to 1.8 meters) long and stocky, with a rounded, conical head and rounded dorsal fin. The Hector's dolphin prefers to stay near shore, and it is this behavior that increases their exposure to deadly fishing gear.

4 STRANDED SEALS AND BEACHED BABIES

To get to the intensive care unit at the New England Aquarium, guests have to step one foot at a time into a shallow pan of disinfectant. Carrying germs into these rooms would make matters worse for the animals temporarily living there—sick and recuperating sea turtles, harbor seals, and other animals rescued from nearby beaches.

The headquarters for the New England Aquarium Marine Animal Rescue team is behind the scenes in a network of hallways and cubbyhole-like rooms where staff and volunteers respond to calls of stranded marine animals along the eastern coast from Maine to Massachusetts.

"We see harbor seal pups in May, and Arctic ice seals in winter," said John Dayton, general curator and director of animal husbandry at the aquarium. Winter tends to be the busy season with mass cetacean strandings and "cold-stunned" sea turtles.

Animals that end up at the aquarium may have encountered an oil spill, toxic material, or a boat's thrashing propeller. They may have swallowed plastic garbage bags or were caught in a fishing net. Some become stranded because of disease or following an attack from a predator. In 1968, when the rescue and rehabilitation program started, they responded to strandings, in part, to find out why marine mammals ended up dead on the beach. "At this point, we know why many of them strand. Now rehabilitation is for the individual animals," said Dayton.

Currently, there are hundreds of rescue-rehabilitation centers that dot the U.S. coastline, an efficient network of professionals and volunteers. When someone calls in a stranding, the staff and volunteers grab the equipment they need. Lining the hallway are transport kennels for seals and stretchers specifically made to fit all sizes of whale and dolphin. Veterinary supplies are also packed into a truck.

A harbor seal pup gets a physical exam at the New England Aquarium by a Marine Animal Rescue team member.

An animal is first examined right on the beach. Sometimes, people call in a stranding when it is simply a harbor seal that has hauled out to bask in the sun. It's normal for seals to spend many hours out of the water. Problems do occur, however, when people interfere with the animal, pet it, or try to feed it. A stressed seal sometimes eats the sand and becomes sick. The rescue team has most of the veterinary and lab equipment it may need to diagnose the problem. Blood samples drawn from a stranded animal tell if it is dehydrated or suffers from an infection—important clues as to why the animal became stranded. The crew checks the animal's respiration, listens for wheezing or coughing, and decides whether or not to take the animal back to the aquarium.

"We try to pick the best candidates for success," said Dayton. "But the staff at the aquarium really push the envelope." The rescue team once brought in harbor porpoises that Dayton thought were dead, and nursed them back to good health.

ALL EYES ON SEAL NUMBER 7

Rehab work offers veterinarians and biologists an opportunity to learn more about a species and to try innovative procedures. "There is so much we don't know about marine mammals," New England Aquarium veterinarian Sonia Mumford said. "It is so rewarding when you try something new and it works."

Seal pup number 7 provided such an opportunity. It was rescued along with seven other harbor seal pups stranded on the coast. The day I visited them at the aquarium they were getting a lesson in lunch. A technician tossed fish into the pool in order to teach them to swim after the fish and eat them. One pup was not catching on and had to be force-fed. One of the rescue and rehab crew members straddled the seal on her knees. She held its mouth open with one hand and stuffed a fish in with the other. Each pup had a number glued to the top of its head for easy identification. Number 7 also had tubes on the top of its head.

"That one has an eye problem," explained Mumford. "Seals are similar to horses. Once they clamp their eyes shut there is no way

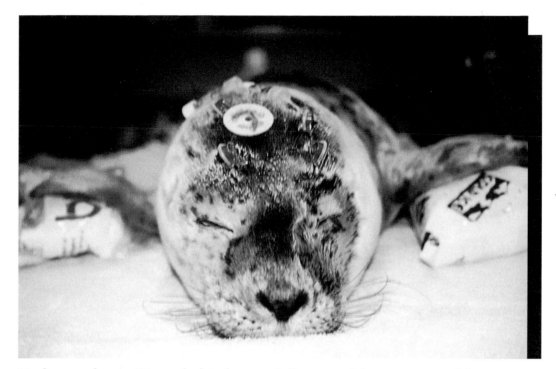

Harbor seal pup #7 needed to be specially treated for an eye problem.

to open them." Tubes were surgically implanted under the eyelids and fastened to the top of its head. The small vials that were attached allowed the veterinarian to administer medication directly to the eye without wrestling with the pup. "This is the first time we have tried this method," she said. There are wild seals that are blind in one eye and very successful, but a totally blind seal would probably not survive. This procedure was important for the success of seal number 7, and also for the veterinarians to know that it was a viable technique that could be used again.

After 14 weeks of eye treatments, number 7, like its pool mates, was released back into the ocean. One measure of how well the rehab crew has done its job is if the animals survive the first 100 days out in the wild. Then they know that the seal has been successful feeding itself. The crew was curious how number 7 would do after such an unusual ordeal, so expert tracker Greg Early fitted it with a satellite tag. Although it appeared the seal was healthy and doing well, it took some very odd trips. "He went as far south as New York Harbor. He went up the Hudson River and was off the end of Long Island when we lost track of him," Early said.

A rare Hawaiian monk seal

A Rare Seal

The Hawaiian monk seal (*Monachus schauinslandi*) is one of the rarest seals in the world. Experts estimate that there are less than 1,400 seals left struggling to survive. These extremely shy pinnipeds are easily disturbed by human interference and have been pushed to the small atolls and islets northwest of Hawaii. They are also threatened by fishing entanglements, pollution, and their own deadly behavior.

There are so few females left that males will "mob" a female in an attempt to mate. Several large males ganging up on a female often leaves her fatally wounded. Injured females are sometimes taken to aquariums for rehabilitation, and young pups are protected from aggressive males by being placed in a fenced enclosure on the beach until they are large enough to be released.

Sometimes rehab work is disappointing, sad, and even uncomfortable, especially when someone must sit in cold water all night keeping an animal's head above water. But when an animal is released it is most rewarding. The crew at the New England Aquarium has rehabilitated pilot whales, white-sided dolphins, harbor seals, harp seals, hooded seals, and harbor porpoises. Dozens of other aquariums and organizations rescue and rehabilitate marine mammals as well. Procedures are different for each species, but the goal is the same: saving marine mammals.

OTTER SCHOOL

Seals at the New England Aquarium get a few fishing lessons, but sea otters at the Monterey Bay Aquarium have their own personal tutor. Young otters usually learn all there is to know from their mothers—how to groom their fur, find food, and ride out rough seas—but most of the sea otters that become stranded are pups separated from their mothers by a storm or other disaster. Orphaned pups that have not learned it all end up on the beach hungry, dehydrated, and sick. The Sea Otter Research and Conservation Program began in 1984 to help these otters return to the wild. "We get, on average, eleven a year," said Andy Johnson, the program director.

Returning even a fraction of them back to their natural habitat is not only humane, but may be vital for the species. At one time more than 20,000 otters swam off the coast of California. Their dense warm fur made them valuable and the target of hunters who brought the population to near extinction in the early 1900s. Today they are protected under the 1972 Marine Mammal Protection Act and the Endangered Species Act. But the sea otter's survival is still viewed as precarious. Their recovery has been very slow, increasing by only 5 percent in past years, peaking in the spring of 1995 at 2,377. There were slightly fewer in the spring of 1999. The decline is attributed to the interaction of several factors. "The population could be slow to recover anyway," said Johnson. "It's a highly populated area, in contact with a lot of environmental contaminants, fisheries, high parasite loads, and severe weather conditions." A major worry is that a single oil spill or other catastrophe could wipe them out. It's a real fear since the California sea otter's refuge is less than 100 miles (161 kilometers) from the nearest oil rig.

Johnson says that raising baby otters is a learning experience—a slow evolutionary process of figuring out what they need at various stages of their development, and how to deliver it.

One method that seems to be working is one-on-one care. Each young pup is assigned two caregivers who work 12-hour shifts so that someone is near them day and night. Otter pups scream and cry for Mom a lot, and their calls for companionship often mean that the caregivers miss lunch or much-needed sleep.

Although these bundles of activity are pet-sized, they are treated as wild animals. The aquarium staff prefers to use the term *caregiver* instead of *surrogate mom*, because as Johnson said, "This relationship that's formed [between caregiver and otter], although it's a close one, is necessary to provide the animal with adequate survival skills so that it can be reintroduced to the wild." To make daily care easier, the staff does give each otter a name (after characters in John Steinbeck novels), but officially the pups are referred to by number.

A week-old pup needs to be fed every two hours like a human baby, with a yummy

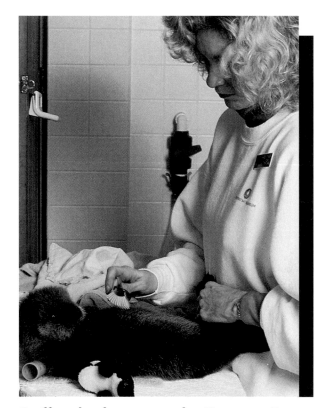

Staff and volunteers at the Monterey Bay Aquarium's Sea Otter Research and Conservation program groom orphaned sea otter pups.

blend of clams, squid, half-and-half, fish oil, fluids, vitamins, and minerals. When they are about three months old, pups are off the milk shakes and eating whole clams, shrimp, mussels, squid, and live crabs.

The next important task is grooming. A caregiver will spend up to four hours a day grooming the fur, an important skill that the pup needs to learn to do for itself once it is back in the chilly ocean. Otters do not have a layer of blubber to keep them warm like other marine mammals do. They rely on air bubbles trapped in their dense fur to keep them insulated from the cold. Without grooming skills, a pup would lose body heat and suffer from hypothermia.

Other otter lessons include wrestling, deep diving, foraging, how to open sea urchins, and learning to ride out rough seas. This means taking them on field trips out into the bay where the young otters get a real sense of what it will be like to live in the ocean. From the beach adjacent to the aquarium, the otter and a caregiver in diving gear plunge into the chilly waters of Monterey Bay. At first, the otters stick close to the divers. But soon, the lure of the wild pulls them farther out. They are encouraged to explore on their own, and no one is sad when an older otter stays out all night. Swimming lessons may last as long as four hours of diving, rolling, and searching the ocean floor for tasty sea urchins, the otters' favorite food.

Wild sea otters spend their days rolling and sliding through the water, taking naps snuggled in a blanket of kelp. They appear to be carefree, but they have all sorts of worries. Although they live within the Monterey Bay National Marine Sanctuary, they are not wholly safe, so each successfully rehabilitated pup helps the species. One adult female that was rehabed and released gave birth the following year. "That was one case that we knew of where we intervened and the population is now up by one," Johnson said.

The program's success rate nearly matches the survival rate of otter pups in the wild. Experts estimate that only 25 percent of the pups survive past the first year. The aquarium keeps tabs on its pups by fitting them with VHF radio tags implanted in their abdomens. Success means that the animal has lived as long, and hopefully longer, than the two-year life of the battery in the transmitter.

Rehabilitating sea otters not only teaches the otter how to survive, but it also teaches people about otter survival. "It's a bit of a snapshot of these animals in the wild," Johnson said. It's a valuable opportunity to handle the otters and gather data on behavior, social structure, diet, health, and the population. Knowledge that may come in handy if the worst case scenario, an oil spill, should ever happen.

A rather distinguished-looking sea otter

Sea Otters (*Enhydra lutris*)

Sea otters are the smallest marine mammals, and are related to river otters, weasels, mink, and badgers. They live among the kelp beds, feeding on shellfish and sea urchins. Its flexible spine and agility allow the sea otter to keep its dense fur clean and fluffed, trapping a layer of air bubbles within its fur in order to stay warm.

Historically, sea otters ranged throughout the Pacific Rim from northern Japan, across the Bering Sea, and south along the California coast. Although some sea otter populations remain strong, others such as the California colony are endangered. The 1998 census recorded 2,114 California sea otters.

5 DATA FROM THE DEAD

A dead manatee floating along the coastline is a stinking 2,000-pound (908-kilogram) laboratory of scientific data. Deciphering that data is the job of pathologists like Tom Pitchford, assistant research scientist at the Marine Mammal Pathobiology Lab in St. Petersburg, Florida.

Pitchford is just one link in an elaborate chain of researchers and volunteers helping manatees and other marine mammals. "It's a network of staff with trucks and trailers, cell phones and pagers distributed around the coastline of Florida to respond to reports of dead and injured manatees. Each field station is within an hour's drive of any reported dead manatee," Pitchford said.

People living in manatee country know that if they see a dead or injured animal, they should call the Florida Marine Patrol hot line. A response team will be dispatched to pick up the carcass. If it is out on the water, for example, a marine patrol will retrieve it and tow it to a boat ramp, where the manatee is loaded onto a trailer the same way a small boat is. The trailer is backed down the ramp and a winch hauls the carcass onto the trailer bed.

Having a quick response time is important, because a dead manatee can decay quickly under the Florida summer sunshine. "Decomposition is the enemy," Pitchford warns. "We want to get the carcass, get it cooled down, and get it to the lab so we can perform lab tests on the animal before the body is altered by the decomposition process." The fresher the body is, the more accurate the information is. Sometimes if the animal can't be moved, a response team will do a necropsy, an autopsy, right where it was found.

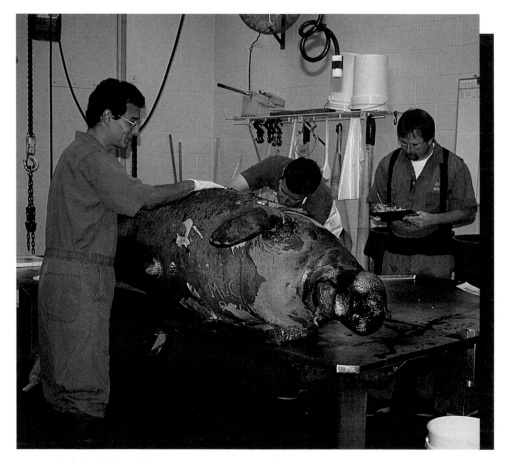

Tom Pitchford bends over a manatee during a necropsy.

At the lab, a 3-ton (2.7-tonne) hoist lifts the manatee from the trailer and places it on a stainless-steel table, where it can be wheeled into the necropsy room. Pitchford and his staff first take photographs of the manatee's scars and markings. These will be compared with the extensive file of manatee photos kept by the Sirenia Project. The body is then scanned for a PIT tag, a Personal Identification Transponder, which is a tiny coded chip that is implanted in previously rescued or captured manatees. These small chips are surgically placed in the shoulder and neck area, and can be "read" by passing a handheld device over the body. A positive reading means that this manatee was caught once before, and has a serial number and a record file that the staff can pull up and review.

"Of course it's sad when we get a manatee that is known to us," Pitchford said. "But we also use that opportunity to maximize our information. We immediately have a life history, and it can direct our necropsy. For example, if the manatee was treated for broken bones, we will look for those healed bones in the necropsy."

A lot of information can also be learned from animals they have never seen before. A necropsy on any rare animal is an important opportunity to learn about it. "At one time we would have had to go out and shoot the animal to find out this information," Pitchford said.

The necropsy team can tell what the animal ate from its stomach contents, learn if it was sick from chemical analysis, and even tell how old the animal was when it died by looking closely at the inner ear. A manatee's ear bone grows in layers each year. Scientists section or slice through the ear bone of the animal and count the rings in the bone, just like a botanist counts the rings on a tree.

If the head is badly damaged and the inner ear bone is missing, then they can rely on a new technique developed at the lab that measures the distance between various bones in the flipper and other parts of the body.

Scientists keep tissue samples, skeletons, and skulls to use in later studies, and to develop new diagnostic techniques that make their job more exact, and gather more information from the carcasses.

A typical necropsy can take anywhere from one hour to half the day depending on the decomposition of the remains. The scientists will spend more time studying a fresh body, because they can collect valuable samples and perform important tests even on a seemingly healthy animal that might have been hit by a boat. This kind of information provides the researchers with vital baseline data about what is normal for an animal of a particular age, and in a particular area—such as what kinds of parasites it normally carries, or what its usual diet is. But the primary focus of a necropsy is to determine cause of death, a process similar to solving a whodunit mystery.

RED ALERT

Over a two-month period in 1996, 149 manatees were reported dead. "It was crazy," Pitchford said. "We're used to one to two bodies a week, but we were picking up five or six a day." On one particularly grim day, 11 dead manatees were reported. Switching to crisis response mode, the team called in extra help from around the country, and temporarily moved the lab to Sanibel Island, closer to the die-off area.

Along the Fort Myers coastline, rafts of dead fish floated up onto the beach, and cetaceans and turtles were found stranded. It was a red-tide event, a natural but deadly phenomenon. Lying dormant in the muck and mud at the ocean's bottom are microscopic organisms called algae that explode into action when weather, food, and other factors are just right. The algae emit toxins that poison fish and are sometimes deadly to marine mammals and humans, and recent research suggests that red-tide events might be increasing due to man-made factors such as agricultural runoff and other pollutants.

Although the researchers suspected a red tide, no one knew why or how the manatees were dying. On the outside, the dead

A mother and calf manatee nuzzle in King's Bay, Crystal River, Florida.

West Indian Manatee (*Trichechus manatus*)

The manatee has been called a sea cow because it is strictly vegetarian, consuming 60 to 100 pounds (27 to 45 kilograms) of sea grass a day. Manatees grow to be more than 3,000 pounds (1,360 kilograms) and 10 feet (3 meters) long, and spend most of their time feeding in shallow coastal waters around Florida, moving to inland rivers and estuaries in the winter. The 1998–1999 winter survey sighted more than 1,800 manatees living in U.S. waters, but they estimate that the total population figure is 2,400.

manatees appeared normal, but necropsies revealed that all the victims had congested lungs, bleeding around the brain, and inflamed nasal passages. By studying the dead animals, Greg Bossart at the University of Florida developed a diagnostic test that could detect the red-tide toxin in tissue samples. The toxin turned out to be a

Manatee bodies are iced to slow decay, before they are hauled back to the Marine Mammal Pathology Lab and examined to find the cause of death.

neurotoxin, which means it attacks the respiratory and nervous systems. It was the first time that such a test had confirmed this kind of natural disaster in manatees.

Although the event was tragic, it taught scientists a lot. Without the bodies of the unfortunate 149 manatees, the test could not have been developed. It has since been used to diagnose the mysterious deaths of other manatees during smaller but no less tragic die-offs. Without the large numbers of dead manatees to alert the public, these smaller events would have gone unnoticed.

LIFESAVING LAWS

Pathology can be a grim job of data collection, but it's also a fascinating field in which scientists can help save animals' lives by changing laws.

"We are constantly looking at the relationship between different factors," Pitchford said. How is age related to different causes of death? Are manatees of a certain age group more susceptible to boat strikes than at other times in their lives? Are females or males more prone to get hit by a boat? Is one gender or age more affected by cold weather? The answers to these kinds of questions ultimately lead to better manatee-friendly laws.

In the state of Florida, there are more than 750,000 boats registered, and more are brought into the state during vacation season. Slow-floating vegetarians lose out against fast boats with sharp propellers. The damage is so prevalent that scientists can individually identify 90 percent of the manatees by scars received from boat collisions.

For more than 27 years, the lab has compiled data supporting the fact that boat collisions are a major cause of death for manatees. This mortality data coupled with telemetry studies that show where the manatees live, and habitat studies that pinpoint prime habitats, have created a clear picture of the areas that should be protected. In 1989, 13 counties were identified for manatee protection and these counties have since adopted new regulations restricting boat speeds in certain waters.

The piece of gill net around this young sea lion's neck will not stretch. Unless conservationists can get it off, the sea lion will be killed as it grows.

Pick It Up!

What we throw away might be just garbage to you, but to a sea turtle or marine mammal it might look like a tasty meal. Our garbage is a death trap for marine life. Discarded cigarettes, fishing hooks, and hair scrunchies have all been pulled from the stomachs of dead manatees. Floating plastic bags look like tasty jellyfish and are eagerly swallowed whole. They clog an animal's digestive system or block the airway, causing the whale or manatee to drown.

One pygmy sperm whale found stranded on the shores of New Jersey had bits of plastic, the cellophane off a box of cigarettes, pieces of a garbage bag, and one whole Mylar party balloon blocking its digestive tract. After the trash was surgically removed, the whale (nicknamed Inky) was rehabilitated by the staff at the National Aquarium in Baltimore and released back to the ocean. But not every animal is so lucky.

The next time you toss a gum wrapper on the ground, think about where it might end up.

THE BOOK OF THE DEAD

Pierre Beland keeps what he calls the Book of the Dead, a solemn record of all the dead beluga whales he has necropsied since 1982. Beland is the senior research scientist with the St. Lawrence National Institute of Ecotoxicology, and has collected more than 180 entries so far.

Just as the records at the Pathobiology Lab in Florida tell the story of life and death among manatees, Pierre Beland's Book of the Dead, his pathology logbook, tells the story of the St. Lawrence beluga whales.

Just 50 years ago, experts estimated that there were between 5,000 to 10,000 belugas in the Gulf of St. Lawrence, but today there are only about 500. Beland's studies revealed some of the reasons why the beluga population declined and why they haven't recovered.

All the whales that Beland tested had one thing in common—abnormally high levels of toxins in their bodies. They contained more than a dozen poisons, including PCBs, DDT, and an insecticide called mirex. By the age of nine, a beluga whale already contains a higher concentration of PCBs than a ship is allowed to carry without a special permit.

Unlike the boat that can unload its cargo, the beluga will double that concentration by the age of 22. After 16 years of life in the St. Lawrence, a beluga's body also contains enough mercury to cause developmental and neurological problems in humans. St. Lawrence belugas have ulcers and lesions not reported in any other cetacean, and the highest cancer rate of any marine mammal—higher than those reported for humans.

These toxins are in the water and the food chain. Belugas eat eels laced with mirex and fish tainted with DDT. The poisons entered the ecosystem from industries and farms upstream in the Great Lakes. The lakes then drain into the St. Lawrence estuary and head out to sea. It is no coincidence that the decline of belugas occurred at the same time the chemical companies were in their heyday.

Ecotoxicologist Pierre Beland and a dead beluga

Beland discovered that the toxins are particularly fatal to whales because they are stored in fat, and whales have a lot of fat in the form of blubber. Pregnant females pass on their accumulated poisons to their calves during pregnancy and through nursing. Each generation starts out with higher levels than the last.

Beland's book of the dead not only reveals the tragic life and death of whales, but also shows us how our way of living has horribly affected the whales, the sea, other animals, and ourselves.

These belugas are rubbing their bellies on the stony river bottom to remove dead skin.

Beluga Whales (*Delphinapterus leucas*)

Belugas are born a dark gray-blue and get whiter as they age. These stocky, beaked whales grow to be 15 feet (4.6 meters) long and usually have thick folds of blubber along their underside or ventral surface. They always appear to be smiling, and are extremely social animals with a wide range of vocalizations. They are benthic feeders, which means they feed on creatures along the bottom of the ocean. Most belugas live in and around the Arctic, with a small remnant population (500 individuals) living in the Gulf of St. Lawrence. There are between 62,000 and 80,000 belugas worldwide.

6 SHARING THE SEAS

A small Chinese river dolphin called the baiji may become extinct before you graduate from high school. It once swam the Yangtze River in the thousands, but today there are fewer than 100. Those that remain spend their days maneuvering through heavy shipping traffic, dodging fishing lines tied with thousands of hooks, and avoiding dynamite blasts, dredging equipment, and other construction activity along the shore.

Unfortunately, attempts to save the baiji have been unsuccessful. The Chinese government created a semi-natural reserve for the dolphins, but capturing and moving the speedy baiji was difficult, and the few that were transferred died. Baiji do not survive long in captivity, and breeding them would require at least 20 pairs of the hard-to-find animals, further depleting the wild population.

Many experts feel that the freshwater dolphin's fate will be sealed with the construction of one of the largest dams in the world, the Three Gorges Dam due for completion in 2009. It will be 607 feet (185 meters) high and 1.2 miles (2 kilometers) wide, holding back a reservoir longer than Lake Superior. It will displace 1.5 million people, flood thousands of acres of wild land, and alter the river habitat forever.

It may be too late for China's baiji, but it's not too late for other marine mammals. Scientists around the world have identified many of the reasons for marine mammal decline. It's up to us to do something about it.

The key to protecting species is protecting habitats, the food they eat, and the water they live in. And that often means changing human behavior and the way we view natural resources. Unfortunately, China's desire for hydroelectric power has won out over the baiji's survival. Will the desire for jet-ski fun defeat the manatee in Florida, or will our taste for seafood win out over fish stocks and the marine mammals that depend on them?

SUSTAINABLE SEAS

The key word in conservation today is sustainability. It means using the earth's resources at a rate that gives the oceans time to replenish. It's easy to look at the oceans and believe that their bounty is limitless. But it's not. Fishermen know this, and have watched their catch dwindle. In less than 30 years, the Atlantic cod catch has fallen by 70 percent, and bluefin tuna by 80 percent. On the other hand, human seafood consumption has grown five times what it was in 1950. Between 1991 and 1995, commercial fleets worldwide pulled in 84 million tons (76,188,000 million tonnes) a year.

The growing need for a shrinking fish stock has pushed fleets into using more and more destructive methods. Gill nets, the world's most common type of commercial fishing gear, stretch a mile or more across the ocean, and drift nets 10 miles (16 kilometers) long float unattended for days. Long liner ships, like spiders, spin out miles of fishing lines fixed with thousands of baited hooks. Mid-water trawlers use nets big enough to swallow the Statue of

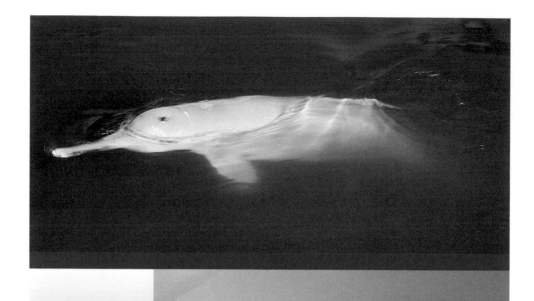

Above: An endangered baiji

Right: An endangered boto

Baiji (*Lipotes vexillifer*)

The baiji is one of only five dolphin species that live solely in a freshwater river system. The others are the boto of the Amazon, the franciscana or La Plata River dolphin, the bhulan or Indus River dolphin, and the susu that lives in the Ganges River system. Because their eyes are not very useful in the murky water, baiji are almost blind. They rely on echolocation, and use their long slender nose to root out fish from the river bottom. Baiji are light gray and grow to be 8 feet (2.4 meters) long. Their Latin name means "the flag bearer who was left behind." Although it refers to the dolphin's white dorsal fin, the name may become the sad reminder of the dolphin that people left behind.

Liberty, and bottom trawlers scrape bare more than 5.8 million square miles (15,000,000 square kilometers) of ocean bottom a year in search of seafood. Bottom trawling is like strip-mining and leaves behind pulverized coral beds and a ravaged ecosystem, ruining vital fish nurseries and destroying an important link in the ocean's food chain.

Each method also catches an enormous amount of bycatch. In the shrimping industry, for example, for every pound (0.45 kilograms) of shrimp caught there are 4 pounds (1.8 kilograms) of unwanted fish and shellfish that are thrown away.

DOLPHIN SAFE

Purse-seine fishing targets herds of dolphins in the search for schools of high-priced tuna that often swim just below. A huge curtain of netting encircles both the tuna and the dolphins and is drawn closed at the bottom like a drawstring purse and hauled aboard.

Prior to the dolphin-safe tuna campaign, thousands of dolphins were also hauled aboard, dead or dying, only to be discarded. In 1986 alone, a reported 133,000 dolphins were killed by the tuna industry off the Pacific Coast.

That figure has dropped to less than 2,000 in 1998 thanks, in part, to Sam LaBudde, a marine biologist, who in the 1980s posed as a cook on a Mexican tuna boat. For six months he secretly videotaped the slaughter. The public was horrified by the images of hundreds of dolphin carcasses piled on deck, and the dolphin-safe tuna campaign began. Pressure from consumers and federal regulations forced the tuna industry to stop using purse-seine nets. Although some countries continue to use the purse-seine method, about 95 percent of the tuna fleets comply, or don't sell their tuna to the United States.

The dolphin-safe tuna campaign changed human behavior. It was a conservation coup and one that hopefully can be repeated. In 1997 the World Wildlife Fund, the largest nonprofit conservation organization, formed a partnership with Anglo-Dutch Unilever Corporation, one of the world's largest buyers of frozen fish and

Sam LaBudde's incredible videotapes have saved thousands and thousands of dolphins.

producer of frozen-fish products. They founded the Marine Stewardship Council, whose mission is to promote sustainable fishing by promoting responsible and environmentally sound fishing practices, which would maintain biodiversity and productivity of marine ecosystems. It would bring together those who stand to gain the most from protecting marine habitats—the fisheries and consumers. With a healthy fish population, the fishermen would continue to earn their living on the water, and consumers would continue to have the seafood that forms an important part of their diet. Marine mammals would also benefit; they would be assured a healthy food supply.

GIVING THE RIGHT WHALE RIGHT-OF-WAY

The southeastern Atlantic Coast from Georgia to Florida is one of the busiest shipping zones in U.S. waters. Tankers and cargo ships loaded with cars, clothing, and raw materials enter the United States through three commercial shipping ports, and naval destroyers, frigates, and nuclear submarines come and go from two active military bases.

These shipping channels crisscross a warm, rich coastal ecosystem perfect for raising young whales, an important nursery for the endangered Northern Atlantic right whale. But for the slow-swimming whales it's like raising their calves in the middle of a freeway. Collisions with ships is the number-one cause of death for

Chris Slay photographed this mother and calf northern right whale during an Early Warning System flight. Ships were warned of the whales and adjusted their directions.

the right whale, whose population numbers less than 300. In 1990, eight right whales died after being hit by ships.

Right whales typically rest on the surface and have not developed defenses against freighters. They do not seem to detect or get out of the way of approaching ships, and their finless backs make them difficult to spot. But there are eyes in the sky that are helping to locate these rare whales as they bask at the surface. It's called the Right Whale Early Warning System (EWS). The Army Corps of Engineers, the Coast Guard, Navy, and National Marine Fisheries Service fund survey flights across the nursing grounds every day (weather permitting) from December through March, when females and calves are in the area.

The EWS flights are conducted by a team of four from the New England Aquarium: one pilot, two observers, and one data recorder. Flying in a grid pattern, they document the presence of right whales as well as sea turtles, sharks, and other marine life. The location of each right whale is radioed to commercial and military traffic controllers who then relay the message to ships in the area, so they can change course or slow down to avoid hitting a whale. It may be working; for 1997 and 1998 there were no collisions in that area.

SANCTUARY AT SEA

It may be impossible to truly protect the whale's habitat in the busy shipping channels of the southeastern Atlantic, but other parts of the ocean have been set aside and designated as sanctuaries. There are 12 marine sanctuaries along the U.S. coast managed by the National Oceanic and Atmospheric Administration (NOAA). Combined, the sanctuaries add up to 18,000 square miles (46,620 square kilometers) of ocean, but it's only a tiny fragment of the total area that the United States claims jurisdiction over.

Unfortunately, a sanctuary is not necessarily a safe place for the marine life that live there. Although drilling, dredging, and dumping of waste is generally prohibited, shipping and fishing are

The Comeback Whale

Back in the 1800s, scores of whaling ships would patrol the waters from California to Mexico looking for the devilfish, the gray whale. When a female and calf were spotted, the whalers harpooned the small calf in order to lure the angry female closer to the ship. They were easy targets. By 1946 the California population of gray whales was nearly extinct, and so they were banned from the hunt. Given a chance to breathe and breed, the gray whales rebounded. In the 1970s whale watchers became the whale watched, as "friendly" gray whales approached small boats and allowed people to scratch their heads. In 1994 scientists estimated that there were 25,000 eastern Pacific gray whales, and judged them fully recovered. The Pacific gray whale became the first marine mammal ever taken off the endangered species list. However, this honor may make the gray whale eligible for the hunt once again.

allowed. Twenty-five miles (40 kilometers) east of Boston, Massachusetts, in Stellwagen Bank National Marine Sanctuary, humpback whales make themselves at home in the summer, and more than 800,000 tourists visit on whale watches each year. It's a 782-square-mile (2,025-square-kilometer) patch of open ocean, but there are no fences or signs that say Keep Out. Environmentalists have voiced their concern that boats go too fast through the sanctuary, increasing the likelihood of a collision. Their fears are not unfounded. Whale-watching boats have struck at least three whales since 1997. Commercial fishing in Stellwagen also continues. One scientist likened the bottom trawling of Stellwagen to clear cutting the rain forests.

A major benefit of the sanctuaries is that they are places where scientific research flourishes, and discoveries are made almost every day. And those discoveries are the backbone of sound conservation policy. Pathologists counted the scars of manatees, and speed limits were instituted. Telemetry trailed the rare right whale, and now both its homes can be protected.

The need to know more about marine mammals increases as the population of some species continues to decline. There are a lot more questions to ask. For example, do right whales sleep or nurse on the surface at certain times of the day more than at others, making them more vulnerable to boat strikes? What is a female monk seal looking for when selecting a beach to raise her pup on, and can we preserve those elements? What factors increase a sea otter pup's chances of survival? Can we clean up the toxins in the beluga's environment? There is a lot more research to be done.

The challenges that conservationists face each day increase as nations lobby to reinstate whaling, the fishing industry develops new and more destructive fishing techniques, and a growing human population flocks to the seashore. But there is something about marine mammals that speaks to the human heart. The manatee's gentleness, the complexity of a dolphin's brain, the cries of an infant sea otter, and the smile of a beluga whale should remind us that we must share the seas.

GLOSSARY

bioacoustics — the scientific study of natural sounds

cetaceans — the group of animals that includes whales, dolphins, and porpoises

echolocation — locating objects and prey by emitting sound waves that are reflected back by the objects

hydrophone — an underwater microphone

necropsy — an examination and autopsy of a dead body

pathology — the study of disease and causes of death

pinniped — the group of animals that includes seals, sea lions, and walruses

red tide — a bloom of toxic algae

sirenia — the group of aquatic herbivores that includes manatees and dugongs

sustainable harvest — using natural resources at a rate equal to the ecosystem's ability to replenish the populations

telemetry — the use of radio devices and other technology to track and monitor animals

FURTHER READING

For more information about marine mammals and how scientists study them, look for these and other resources:

Ackerman, Diane. *The Moon by Whale Light.* New York: Vintage Books, 1991.

Beland, Pierre. *Beluga, a Farewell to Whales.* New York: Lyons and Burford Publishers, 1996.

Carwardine, Mark. *Whales, Dolphins and Porpoises.* London: Kindersley, 1995.

Clark, Margaret Goff. *The Vanishing Manatee.* New York: Cobblehill Books, 1990.

Connor, Richard C. *The Lives of Whales and Dolphins.* New York: Henry Holt & Co., 1994.

INTERNET INFORMATION
Florida Marine Research Institute at www.fmri.usf.edu
Monterey Bay Aquarium at www.mbayaq.org
National Marine Fisheries Service at www.nmfs.gov
New England Aquarium at www.neaq.org
        (check out their Electronic Newsletter called *Seabits*).
Sea World at www.seaworld.org
WhaleNet at http:whale.wheelock.edu
World Wildlife Fund at www.wwf.org

INDEX